Original title:
Beneath the Ocean's Skin

Copyright © 2025 Creative Arts Management OÜ
All rights reserved.

Author: Sebastian Whitmore
ISBN HARDBACK: 978-1-80587-235-1
ISBN PAPERBACK: 978-1-80587-705-9

## Mysterious Waterways

In the depths where fish wear hats,
Mermaids dance with flapping bats,
An octopus spins a disco ball,
While sea turtles play beach volleyball.

Crabs wear sunglasses, looking fine,
Tangled in seaweed, feeling divine,
A dolphin jokes, "Who needs a boat?"
As whales send messages in a note.

Starfish hold talent shows at night,
With jellyfish providing the light,
Clownfish tell jokes that make you guffaw,
While sea cucumbers just sit in awe.

Anemones wave, they're quite the scene,
In underwater realms, where all's routine,
So if you dive, don't wear a frown,
There's laughter and joy in the ocean's town.

**The Fluidity of Dreams.**

In a world where fish can skate,
Octopuses dance on plates.
Seaweed grows like tangled hair,
Crabs in tuxedos quite the flair.

Sharks do the cha-cha, so they say,
Whales burst into song, all day.
When jellyfish throw a rave at night,
You can't resist that glowing light.

## Whispers of the Deep

The clams are gossiping quite loud,
While squids perform, they draw a crowd.
Eels in suits of electric green,
Make faces that are rather obscene.

The sea cucumber sings a tune,
Riding waves on a bubble balloon.
Dolphins crack jokes, what a delight,
In a wacky underwater night!

## Secrets in the Abyss

Fish flip burgers on the grill,
While starfish plot their next big thrill.
A treasure chest sings off-key,
And mermaids laugh in jubilee.

The octopus handed out blue drinks,
While pufferfish wear flashy blinks.
Down in the depths, fun's the decree,
As sea life waltzes with glee!

## Tides of Tranquility

The sand dollars tell silly tales,
While crabs flip coins for playful wails.
Coral sways to a funky beat,
As lobsters breakdance on their feet.

Sea turtles marathon with flair,
Jellyfish float without a care.
In this realm of laughter and cheer,
Who knew anemones held so dear?

## **Between the Fathoms**

A fish in a tux, oh what a sight,
Dancing with seaweed, oh what a fright.
Jellyfish jitterbugs, glowing with glee,
Making strange shadows, all carefree.

Crabs in a conga, snap to the beat,
Starfish spin tales, oh what a feat!
Seahorses giggle, twirling in style,
An octopus winks, and all chuckle a while.

## Aquatic Parables

A clam told a tale of a pearl so grand,
But it turned out to be just a grain of sand.
The dolphins were rolling, laughing with pride,
As a turtle forgot where he parked his ride.

The anglerfish grinned, with light in his smile,
He caught an old boot—now that's quite a trial!
While a lazy old sponge took a nap in between,
Waking up only for a snack feast unseen.

## The Silent Call

In the depths where the sea cucumbers yawn,
A whale's got a crush, but it's widely withdrawn.
The krill are all giggling, quite light on the toes,
As a sea lion barks out a song that just glows.

But lost in the bubbles, a grouper is glee,
Swimming in circles, playing hide and seek.
The ocean might whisper, with currents that twirl,
Yet all that it finds is a dogfish with curls.

## Siren's Silent Soliloquy

A siren once sung, but lips were quite sealed,
Her fishy friends snickered, 'Her fate is revealed!'
With a wink and a wink, she tossed her long hair,
But caught in the kelp, she marooned in despair.

Grouper said, 'Dear, you're a real work of art,
But forgetting the tune makes it hard to take part!'
With seaweed confetti, they cheered her on loud,
As the bubbles of laughter made up for the crowd.

## Beneath the Surface's Whisper

In a sea of bubbles, fish do dance,
They giggle and wiggle, take a chance.
A crab offers snacks with pinch and squeeze,
While octopuses juggle with the greatest ease.

A dolphin tells jokes that really flop,
The seaweed starts laughing, can't make it stop.
A turtle in glasses reads a big book,
Says, 'This is better than any old nook!'

## Secrets of the Sand and Sea

Waves whisper secrets, but who would know?
A clam with a pearl puts on quite the show.
Starfish hold meetings, take secret votes,
While sandy folks build their tiny boats.

Seahorses giggle at their silly tails,
They ride on the currents like happy trails.
The hermit crab grumbles about his last shell,
"It was cozy, but now it smells like a well!"

### The Lure of the Abyssal

Down in the depths where the sunlight's shy,
A fish wears a hat, oh my, oh my!
Anglerfish grins with a glowy hook,
"Join my party, come take a look!"

Squid with a pen writes underwater jokes,
While anemones play with giggling folks.
The deep-sea divers don't know what's near,
Attracting odd fish with their strange career!

## **Tidal Reveries**

When tides start to dance, you might just see,
An octopus moonwalking, wild and free.
The tidal pools laugh, and crabs start to cheer,
"Let's make this a party; everyone's here!"

A sea lion lounges, wearing cool shades,
Pondering life on his sun-drenched glades.
Jellyfish twirl, a bubble ballet,
In the party of waves, who'd want to stay away?

## Fables in the Foam

The jellyfish danced, oh what a sight,
In glittering gowns, they twirled with delight.
A crab shouted, "Hey, watch your sting!",
As seaweed went flying, what chaos they bring!

The fish wore their masks, a carnival show,
With bubbles for laughter, they all stole the flow.
A dolphin, quite jokey, did flip and did spin,
"Pack your fin! Let's race! I'm going to win!"

## Heartbeat of the Deep

The octopus giggled, eight arms in a knot,
Chasing a shrimp that was quick on the spot.
They laughed through the currents, jolly and spry,
While starfish just grumbled, too sleepy to try.

A turtle named Ted was rolling a die,
For bingo with clams, oh my, oh my!
He lost every round but cheered with a grin,
"Next time, dear friends, I'm sure I will win!"

## Tales from the Blue Depths

A whale told a riddle that swam in the tide,
"Why did the clam get a fish for a bride?"
The catfish all chuckled, their scales all aglow,
"Because she didn't mind being shy in a show!"

Anemones giggled, swaying with glee,
As the grouchy old eel screamed, "Get off my sea!"
But all of them knew, it was just for the fun,
In their frolicsome world, where laughter's the sun!

## The Glimmering Darkness

In shadows of coral, a party was planned,
With shrimp as the DJs, and clams making sand.
"Let's boogie!" they cheered, with a wink and a nod,
As a starry-eyed anglerfish flashed a façade.

But what's that commotion? A sea horse got stuck,
In a net made of seaweed, oh what bad luck!
"Don't fret!" called the shrimp, "You're in for a treat,
You'll dance on the reef, now isn't that neat?"

## Oceanic Whispers

In the depths, where fish do chat,
A crab in a tux, who looks quite fat.
He dances with a jelly, does a silly twist,
While seaweed giggles, it can't resist.

A dolphin jumps with a toothy grin,
"I'm the king of the waves, let the fun begin!"
The clownfish chuckles, quite the prank,
And octopus joins with a laugh, how frank!

Starfish tell tales with sticky tips,
Waving to friends in aquatic quips.
They sip from shells, a bubbly brew,
In the world below, laughter's true hue.

So if you dive and hear a song,
Don't be alarmed, you'll find where you belong.
Just follow the giggles through coral right,
For humor reigns in the sea's delight.

## Ephemeral Flora of the Abyss

In gardens of seaweed, giggles bloom,
Where mermaids twirl in a watery room.
A flower pot fish plays hide and seek,
With a wink and a splash, so unique!

Anemones sway to the jellyfish beat,
While crabs tell jokes with those tiny feet.
A flower that bursts with laughter and cheer,
Makes the ocean's depths feel like a fairground here.

Seahorses trot in their fancy dance,
As plankton party in a tiny romance.
They blow bubbles in a sparkling whorl,
Creating a frothy fairy-tale swirl.

So peek at the flora, oh what a sight,
Each petal a chuckle, so airy and light.
In the world of the waves, joy is the key,
Where flora dance freely in jubilant spree.

## Secrets in the Salty Air

Under waves, secrets flutter and play,
A fish with a mustache steals the day.
He whispers to shells about the latest scoop,
While clams perform jigs and join in the loop.

A sea turtle spins while spinning a yarn,
About treasures lost, yet no cause for alarm.
The gulls overhead chuckle and squawk,
As cod start a dance, doing the clock!

Crabs share gossip over sandy small pies,
While shrimp wear their hats, oh what a surprise!
They toast with a splash of the briny delight,
And sing silly songs through the day and night.

So if you should wander where salty winds sway,
Remember the secrets that fish like to say.
For laughter's the treasure, the pearl to be found,
In the currents of fun where joy does abound.

## Twilight in the Tide

As the sun dips low, the water glows,
A squid in a bowtie strikes a pose.
He boasts of his dance on a floor made of sand,
While the clowns of the reef clap their hands.

The moonlit waves ripple with giggles and spark,
Where sea stars twirl till the cheeky dawn hark.
"Join us!" they cry with a wave in their glee,
While barnacles bob to the jolly decree.

A fish parade marches in silly attire,
With bubbles and laughter, they never tire.
The tide pools laugh, sharing tales of the night,
In this twilight place, everything feels right.

So come to the shore as the day bids adieu,
In the twilight's embrace, there's always a view.
With smiles and fun riding the tide's friendly hand,
It's a joyful gala in this watery land.

## The Enigma of Aquatic Shadows

In a world where fish can giggle,
And clams can crack a joke,
The seaweed shakes with laughter,
As starfish do the poke.

Octopuses play hide and seek,
While dolphins dance a jig,
A crab pinches for a laugh,
With moves that are quite big.

The turtles race in silly ways,
Trying hard to win,
But bloated fish just float right by,
With grins that make them grin.

Jellyfish waltz in squid-like grace,
With hats atop their heads,
Each wave a playful tickle,
From friends in ocean beds.

## Whims of the Tidal Whisper

The tide tells jokes to seashells near,
   As surfers tumble down,
  With barrel rolls and goofy grins,
    In waves that spin them round.

A fish who thought he was a dog,
    Fetches rocks with glee,
While sea cucumbers giggle soft,
     At his playful spree.

The playful kraken spins about,
    With arms that are a mess,
Making whirlpools of delight,
Then asks, "Was that my dress?"

Corals wave like jolly fools,
   In colors bright and loud,
As minnows giggle, swimming by,
   In laughter's playful crowd.

## Harmonies from the Depths

In the depths where bubbles rise,
A concert starts to play,
With fish that sing in silly tones,
In quite a fishy way.

The eel's electric symphony,
Brings tunes from fins and tales,
While crabs conduct this underwater,
With rhythm in their scales.

A whale who thinks he's karaoke,
Belts songs of great renown,
While clownfish chuckle in delight,
At his melodious crown.

The sea anemones sway and groove,
To beats of coral songs,
As laughter bubbles through the waves,
Like a chorus of sea throngs.

## Beneath the Blue Veil

In waters filled with silly sights,
The fishes wear their hats,
While sea stars laugh at sea cows' jokes,
Oh, how the ocean chats!

The otters slide on glimmering rocks,
With laughter in each splash,
While heartiest laughs are bubble-burst,
In a saltiest giddy thrash.

The shrimp make puns as bubbles rise,
In patterns soft and round,
While sea turtles do the twist,
To beats they're all spellbound.

With every wave a punchline thrown,
And laughter rolling free,
In this whimsical watery realm,
It's all one big "Whee!"

## Odyssey of the Mystic Waves

In the depths, a fish with flair,
Wears a top hat, with great care.
He dances near a pearly shell,
Complaining about his fishy smell.

A crab dons shades, struts with pride,
In his beach chair, he takes a ride.
The sea turtles surf, oh what a sight,
Waving at dolphins, all feeling right.

A jellyfish jelly, on a slice of bread,
Served to the seahorses, laughing instead.
They giggle and wiggle, a slippery crew,
Sipping seaweed smoothies, who knew?

At sunset, the laughter rises and swells,
With octopuses sharing their silly tales.
A party of plankton, wild and free,
Under the waves, jovial glee.

# Beneath Rippling Surface

A clam with pearls has fashion sense,
Winks at a squid, such confidence.
The starfish tries a moonlit dance,
While bubbles pop, they take a chance.

A pufferfish floats, looking quite grand,
Wearing a crown made of seaweed strand.
A prancing shrimp in a tutu twirls,
Making all the sea snails do dizzy swirls.

The sea cucumbers start a rock band,
With conch shells forming a kicking hand.
The audience? Anemones in a line,
Swaying and dancing, oh so divine!

A kraken's caught on a TikTok reel,
Strumming currents, it's quite the deal.
With underwater memes circulating fast,
Surfing the waves, making memories last.

## Secrets Among the Undertow

In the shadows, a seahorse pranks,
Blowing bubbles, filling tanks.
He tickles a flounder with a fin so sly,
While laughing out loud, they both fly high.

An octopus wears mismatched shoes,
He slips and trips while sharing news.
With eight long limbs, a clumsy dance,
Making the fish all take a chance.

A whale squeaks jokes, a comedian's dream,
While clam shells clap, a fabulous team.
The shrimp form a band and play so loud,
Their underwater tunes make them proud.

A parade with a dolphin, oh what a sight,
Twirling and spinning, oh so light.
Under currents, laughter echoes anew,
Seas of joy, where the silliness grew.

## Ocean's Unseen Lullaby

In the waves, a sleepy seal,
Sings to a clownfish, a vibrant meal.
Dreaming of bubbles floating by,
While a seagull croons a lullaby.

A hermit crab finds a cozy shell,
Turns it into a hotel, oh so swell!
The guests are coral, colorful and bright,
Sharing stories till the moonlight.

A starry night transforms the sea,
As turtles glide, so gracefully.
The underwater critters hum away,
End of the fun, the end of the play.

With twilight serenades in the dark,
Cuddled close, even sharks find a spark.
Underneath the waves, dreams begin,
In this ocean realm, laughter's never thin.

## The Language of Saltwater

Fish gossip in bubbles,
Crabs dance in the sand.
Octopuses juggle treasures,
Seashells rise to expand.

Jellyfish float like balloons,
Laughing with currents' jest.
Starfish play poker at noon,
While sea turtles take a rest.

Mermaids sing silly tunes,
With seaweed in their hair.
They invite you to join in,
But watch out for the glare!

Underwater, jokes are cheerfully spun,
Blowing bubbles, oh what fun!
When laughter swims in the tide,
In this world, you can't hide.

## Mysteries of the Deep Blue

Deep in the blue, what a sight,
Squirrels with fins take flight.
Anglerfish with lamps so bright,
Though they scare, they're a delight.

Where seahorses wear tiny hats,
The seaweed dances around the mats.
Dolphins cracking jokes like spats,
In this world, nothing falls flat!

Giant squids have ink fights,
Making pages of watery writes.
Each stroke causes chuckled heights,
In the dark, they're comedic sights.

The deep blue glimmers with smiles,
Underwater jokes span the miles.
With every splash and playful dance,
The ocean's secrets find their chance.

## Ripples of the Unknown

Ripples giggle and spin around,
As fish swim upside down.
Starfish tell tales of old,
While barnacles sit quite bold.

The tide pulls pranks on the shore,
Where waves tickle while they roar.
Little crabs making a dash,
While all the clams share a bash.

Turtles float with a crooked grin,
While schools of fish turn with a spin.
A dance-off breaks out with zeal,
Using kelp as a fancy wheel.

Each ripple a jest, they cannot hide,
In this laughter, they take pride.
With every wave's soft caress,
Ocean's mystery feels like a jest.

## **The Hidden Abyss**

In waters deep, secrets abound,
Fish tell jokes with a playful sound.
Eels doing stand-up routines,
In a sea of quirky scenes.

Down in the gloom, echoing laughs,
Bubble parties with giggling staffs.
Crabs with sunglasses and flippers,
Navigating through laughter's zippers.

Sea cucumbers with witty lines,
Worms doing limbo beneath the pines.
Even the rocks can't keep a straight face,
In this quirky, watery place.

The abyss dips deep, but fun is near,
With each splash, joy appears.
In the shadows where mischief plays,
The hidden depths have funny ways.

## The Abyssal Symphony

In a jellyfish's dance, a wiggly sway,
A crab takes a bow, in its own funny way.
A sea turtle chuckles, with an elegant glide,
While seahorses gossip on a colorful ride.

The octopus plays maracas with flair,
While fish act like ninjas, prancing with care.
Anemones giggle, tickling the tide,
As mermaids throw parties, where laughter is wide.

Starfish are star-struck, under disco lights,
Hosting underwater shows, oh what delightful sights!
Clams applaud loudly, as pearls take the floor,
While shrimps break the ice, telling jokes to the score.

In the depths, a chorus of vibrant delight,
With bubbles and giggles, they dance through the night.
The big fish just snickers at the silly ballet,
As tides raise the curtain, on the show of the day.

## Currents of Forgotten Tales

In the swirl of the waves, a tale starts to float,
A narwhal with glasses, reading from a boat.
With dolphins as jesters, leaping around,
A sea lion laughs, as it tumbles down bound.

A grouper and flounder share fishy old lore,
While a clam cracks up, at the punchline's core.
The currents all giggle as stories collide,
Creating a ruckus where mysteries hide.

Tales of mermaids who tripped on their fins,
Or crabs who played poker without any wins.
The seaweed sways, joining this spree,
As bubbles burst forth, with laughter so free.

In the depths, a humor that never grows old,
With secrets and smiles, and stories retold.
Every splash is a laugh, every swirl a delight,
In currents where whimsy sets the ocean alight.

## **Beneath the Surface**


Under shadows of kelp, in gardens of green,
A fish throws a fit, for being so keen.
With wiggles and giggles, it struts down the hall,
While shrimp on the sideline just chuckle and call.

A flounder complains, it's just not fair,
While octopuses roll, in a game of hot air.
The sea cucumbers laugh, what a sight to behold,
As underwater jokes start to unfold.

A whale hums a tune, a beat out of time,
With starfish and sea urchins, creating a rhyme.
The barnacles tap to the rhythm so sweet,
As seaweed sways in a humorous beat.

Down in the depths, where laughter runs free,
The quirkiest creatures make jokes endlessly.
Amongst the corals, a riot of cheer,
Creating a world where the punchlines are clear.

## The Tranquil Below

In peaceful reflections where the humor is light,
A seahorse spills secrets in the soft moonlight.
With bubbles of laughter rising to play,
Even the clownfish can't help but sway.

A gentle tide teases, it's all in good fun,
As crabs make a dash, but still lose the run.
The urchins all poke, with quips to be shared,
In gardens of peace, where the mischief isn't spared.

Starry-eyed fishes chase dreams in their sleep,
While whispers of giggles from sand grains do creep.
The sea floor, a stage, for the odd and the wry,
With jokes floating freely, and laughter nearby.

So gather ye round, in this tranquil domain,
Where jesters of water play silly like rain.
In currents of calm, hilarity flows,
An enchanted abyss where humor still grows.

## Gems of the Deep

In the depths where sea cucumbers roam,
Crabs wear their shells like fancy chrome.
The fish throw a party, a dance on the floor,
While octopi juggle, leaving us wanting more.

With bubbles and giggles, the starfish cheer,
A conch shell DJ spins tunes we can hear.
In this underwater fiesta, lose all your cares,
As seahorses breakdance, defying all pairs.

Jellybeans wobble, they bounce and they sway,
While lobsters serve snacks on this wild buffet.
The treasure's not gold, but a jellyfish's grin,
As the squids shoot ink and the fun's about to begin!

So dive down, my friend, to this wacky retreat,
Where the gems of the ocean are funny and sweet.
Come witness the laughter, a splash of delight,
In this realm of the silly, everything's bright!

## The Ocean's Hidden Heart

In a clam's little house where secrets reside,
A lobster sips tea, with manners and pride.
The fish whisper tales of a magical start,
From the depths of this ocean, the joy is an art.

Turtles race snails, but the snails win each time,
While the seaweed performs its own funky rhyme.
Seahorses giggle, with their heads held up high,
In the hidden heart, levity can't die.

A pufferfish grins, wearing glasses so round,
While sea anemones wiggle and clown around.
A dolphin flips tricks, ever slick with his style,
Creating announcements that bring on a smile.

So lie back in the currents, let laughter take part,
In this whimsical world, feel the ocean's heart.
The wonders within, where laughter flows free,
Life's a comedy act, beneath the sea!

## **A Dance of Marine Shadows**

In the dim-lit realm where shadows play tricks,
The fish do the twist, with their very own flicks.
Eels slide on by, they've got moves oh so sleek,
While the crabs keep the beat, in this oceanic peek.

Coral reefs shimmer with sparkles and flair,
As clownfish don stripes and show off their hair.
The sea turtles trot, looking cool as can be,
In a dance of shadows, wild and free!

With a flip and a flap, watch the flounder take flight,
While a whale's in the back, bringing thunder and light.
Their rhythm is catchy, the currents all swing,
As the ocean itself seems to giggle and sing.

So come, twirl and swirl in this watery ball,
Where shadows and laughter are the best fun of all.
The dance of the deep is a sight to behold,
Filled with joy, silliness, and treasures untold!

## Lament of the Forgotten Waters

In the forgotten depths where the old seaweed groans,
A fish sings a ballad, accompanied by bones.
Once grand and so lively, now silence stands still,
But the humor still bubbles, against all goodwill.

A sea snail lamenting, it drags its old shell,
While the clams tell their stories, not one sounds real well.

A dolphin's a comedian, cracking up all,
Meanwhile sea stars still struggle to crawl.

The jellyfish float, with no worries at all,
While the seahorses try to gracefully sprawl.
Though waters feel forgotten, funny tales still thrive,
In this secretive realm where spirits come alive.

So raise a glass made of kelp, give a cheer for the lost,
In the lament of the deep, it's laughter, not frost.
For even forgotten can bring forth a grin,
In the depths of the sea, where the laughter begins!

## Mysteries of the Sunken World

Deep down where the bubbles burst,
Fish wear hats and sing their verse.
Clams trade shells for fashion tips,
While octopuses plan their trips.

Treasure chests filled with old socks,
As crabs in tuxedos dance on rocks.
Mermaids giggle at human fails,
Their laughter echoes through the gales.

Jellyfish float with such grace,
Inviting all for a silly race.
They jive and wiggle, oh so spry,
While turtles shout, "You can't catch my eye!"

Pirates chase their missing loot,
But find only eels in a big old boot.
Their stories fade like the ocean spray,
In this world where the fish play all day.

## Lurkers in the Twilight Zone

In the shadows, where creatures hide,
A fish in a clown costume took a ride.
With big red shoes and a silly grin,
He boogied hard, let the fun begin!

Ghost sharks tell tales of lost fish fries,
While lurking squids wear clever disguise.
A goofy seal plays peek-a-boo,
Singing songs of what humans do.

Beneath the waves, it's a party spree,
Where fish have more style than you and me.
They throw seaweed confetti high,
Giggling as the jellyfish fly.

In this realm where shadows creep,
Even the ocean's secrets leap.
With a wink and a nod, they all agree,
Life's more fun when you're just a little silly.

## **Entwined with the Currents**

Currents swirl, a dance divine,
Fish samba as they sip on brine.
They spin and twist with flowing grace,
In this underwater, wacky race.

Sea turtles wear shades, looking cool,
While seahorses build a tiny school.
They teach young fry the art of fun,
To wiggle and giggle under the sun.

Eels with charm, stop just to chat,
While crabs rally 'round for a hat.
With shells that shine like glittery stars,
They celebrate life, forgetting their scars.

As bubbles rise to the ocean's top,
There's no rush, there's no stop.
Join the fun, let nothing be grim,
In currents, oh, let your laughter swim!

## The Silent Embrace of Water

Water hides secrets, light as a feather,
Where fish play cards in stormy weather.
Anemones giggle, waving hello,
Enticing everyone for a fun show!

Clownfish jesters make quite a scene,
With tiny crowns, they reign like queens.
Their bubble-blowing skills would impress,
A seaweed fiesta, no time for stress!

The dolphins steal the spotlight, dear,
Whistling jokes for all to hear.
While deep-sea creatures share silly fears,
Of what happens when they look in mirrors!

So raise a fin to the laughter below,
In watery realms where fun always flows.
With every splash and every blink,
Let's toast to the sea with a wink!

## Creatures of the Midnight Realm

In the deep where the sea turtles groove,
Octopuses dance, their limbs in a move.
Jellyfish jiggle, oh what a sight,
Glowing like lamps in the depths of night.

Starfish giggle, they tickle each other,
Sea cucumbers say, 'Don't bother, don't bother!'
Crabs wear top hats, they strut with pride,
As fish throw confetti and party inside.

Sharks wear shades while they sip on sea tea,
Throwing wild parties, so fancy and free.
Dolphins flip pancakes, what a strange dish,
While schools of fish blend in for a swish.

Eels juggle shells, a slippery show,
As clownfish giggle, with smiles all aglow.
In this twilight where laughter runs deep,
Fishy-fun antics, a secret we keep.

## **Choreography of the Currents**

The waves are dancing, with bubbles a-bounce,
  While seahorses twirl, giving it a flounce.
  Coral reefs shake, with rhythm and cheer,
  As clownfish pop up with a hearty jeer.

Anemones sway, their tendrils like hands,
  Ballet in blue, it's a sight that expands.
  Surfers of sound, they glide with such flair,
While fish in top hats groove without a care.

Crabs in a conga, they march to the beat,
While whales serenade with songs oh so sweet.
  In this watery dance, all worries depart,
  With nature's rhythm, the ocean's true heart.

Starfish do the cha-cha, with shells in a spin,
  And mermaids join in, letting the fun begin.
The choreography flows, it's a grand swirling scene,
  Where humor and laughter keep the currents keen.

## Reflections in the Dark

In the quiet abyss where the shadows play,
Fish tell their tales in a glimmering way.
Mirrors of water, where giggles collide,
Shiny scales flashing, there's nowhere to hide.

A crab with a monocle surveys from his rock,
While whispers of laughter tickle the clock.
Turtles tell stories, with a wink and a grin,
Of mermaids who trip in their sequined fin.

Glimmers of silver, where jokes intertwine,
Fish joke of pearls like they're drinking fine wine.
Fathoms of hilarity echo around,
In the dark, where the punchlines are found.

Bubbles are giggles and echoes galore,
As creatures of darkness play games to explore.
When the twilight descends and the jokes start to flow,
Reflections of laughter in this deep, gentle glow.

## Voices in the Siren's Call

From the rocks, a chorus, they giggle and coo,
Siren song echoing, it's a fun rendezvous.
Tales of lost ships turn from fables to laughter,
With each bubbly note, a dance they're after.

A mermaid with curls sings of fishy delights,
While schools of fish play hide-and-seek in the lights.
With shells as their instruments, music abounds,
As the ocean's laughter in harmony sounds.

Tritons play trumpets, with scales all a-shine,
Crabs tap their claws to the rhythm divine.
The waves are the stage, where the fish sing and shout,
In the depths, where the fun never seems to pout.

Waves swirl in delight, as jokes take their flight,
Making mischief until the last sliver of light.
In the sea's jovial embrace, they call out with glee,
The funniest voices beneath the blue sea.

## Ghosts of the Deep

In the depths where the fish often play,
A pirate's hat floats, quite far away.
The seaweed dances, a comical sight,
While jellyfish jiggle in moonbeams of light.

An octopus searches for snacks like a chef,
Spinning his plates, he's a culinary ref.
Shrimp do the cha-cha, all twirling around,
Next to a clam whose secret's profound.

A whale with a smile sings tunes in the blue,
His songs tickle turtles; they chuckle and coo.
With bubbles as chorus, they frolic and dive,
In this goofy ballet, they're totally alive.

So if you find treasure, just don't be alarmed,
For mermaids and dolphins are surely charmed.
In this realm of laughter, where oddities gleam,
Join in the fun; it's a fishy daydream.

## An Odyssey in Waves

Upon the crest where seagulls all shout,
A crab tells a tale, and he's never in doubt.
With pincers all waving, he gives quite a cheer,
As starfish applaud from their benches by the pier.

The ocean's a circus, with seals on parade,
Wearing sunglasses big, and they're never afraid.
A dolphin goes surfing on driftwood so grand,
While clam shells all clap with a thud and a band.

The waves give a wink, then splash with a grin,
As fish join the fun, letting laughter begin.
A crab with a feather duster stops by,
Say, "Watch how I swab, I'm the swellest of guys!"

When twilight descends, they all gather tight,
To share in the stories of day turned to night.
With a flick of a fin, they bow and they cheer,
For the ocean's adventure, the best time of year.

**Dreams Carried on the Tide**

On a swell so smooth where the sea turtles glide,
A whale throws a party, it's quite the wild ride.
With cakes made of kelp and a punch of sea foam,
The fish do a shuffle; it feels like home.

A crab in a tuxedo performs for the crowd,
He juggles the seashells, and they cheer very loud.
Anemones giggle at jokes from the rays,
Tickled by laughter, they dance through the waves.

A jellyfish floats in a disco-ball hue,
With lights that flicker, it's a vibrant view.
Seahorses twirl, with ribbons in tow,
While snails do the worm in the shimmering glow.

As dawn approaches, the bubbles pop free,
And echoes of laughter swirl round in the sea.
When the tide rolls away, stories drift far,
But the joy of that night shines like a bright star.

## Secrets of the Sea Floor

Down at the bottom, where oddities hide,
A mermaid insists on a whimsical ride.
With a treasure map drawn on a flounder's back,
They search for a snack, but it's all just a snack!

The squid plays the trombone, a jazz so alive,
While fishes in bowties reel in the vibe.
They shimmy and shake as they groove on the sand,
From crabs in a conga, to dolphins so grand.

An eel in a top hat serves cocktails with flair,
While clams tell tall tales at their fancy affair.
With pearls as their prizes, they gossip and toast,
To the laughter and fun, and the friendships they boast.

So if you hear giggles from the depths of the sea,
Know it's just a party, as wild as can be.
Where secrets are buried, and friendship's the prize,
With chuckles and bubbles that rise through the skies.

## Fragments of Coral Memories

In a world where fish wear hats,
A crab dances madly, all in spats.
Old octopuses tell tales so grand,
While snails host parties with a conch band.

Sea turtles hitch rides, oh what a sight!
They'll take you to depths and give you a fright.
Jellyfish float with grace and glee,
While seahorses tell jokes, just wait and see!

## **Serenade of the Submerged**

A clownfish waits for its time to shine,
Making faces while sipping on brine.
Starfish hand out snacks and play their flutes,
While anemones wear polka dot suits.

The seaweed sways, a funky jig,
Crabs play tag, and not one is big.
Dolphins all laugh, they splash and spin,
Kicking up bubbles, they wear goofy grins.

## **Veils of Aquatic Dreams**

Angelfish gossip about the day's news,
While porcupine puffers blow up like balloons.
A walrus reads poems under the moon,
And clownfishes hum a silly tune.

In this underwater kingdom, all are jesters,
Where blue crabs join in as ringmasters.
Lionfish pose like fashion stars,
While turtles argue over who's won the wars.

## The Depths' Grasp on Time

Time spins around like a fish on a reel,
With mermaids that giggle, their laughter a squeal.
The sand dollars dance, all wearing their best,
While electric eels give jokes a good test.

A deep-sea diver trips on a shrimp,
Falling in laughter, his buoy's on the limp.
But the deep blue chuckles, with waves that roll,
For here in the depths, joy swallows the soul.

## Where Stars Meet Water


Fish wear hats and dance at night,
They twirl and spin, oh what a sight!
Jellyfish play chess with seashells near,
While octopuses juggle with no fear.

Crabs tell jokes with pinchers wide,
Seahorses giggle, unable to hide.
The moonlight sparkles like confetti gold,
As waves whisper tales that never get old.

Starfish sing ballads, silly and sweet,
In an underwater world, hard to beat.
They laugh at bubbles that float up high,
While turtles munch on seaweed pie.

When the tide goes out, the fun's not done,
As dolphins surf, leaping for fun.
Under the waves, joy does not cease,
Where laughter is endless, and all find peace.

## Lullabies of the Tides

The ocean's lullaby is a giggly sound,
With barnacles playing, they gather around.
A dolphin's laugh is a soothing song,
As waves dance lightly all night long.

Mussels hold hands in a wavy embrace,
While seaweed sways in a funny race.
The crabs softly serenade the moon,
As the tide provides the perfect tune.

Bubble-blowers sing with glee,
Tickling the fish as they float by free.
Anemones wiggle in a jolly way,
While plankton join in on a wild ballet.

As midnight falls and the stars peek through,
The ocean chuckles, "How do you do?"
With a sprinkle of laughter, the sea drifts away,
Lulling the world till the break of day.

## The Invisible Kingdom

A kingdom of giggles lies out of view,
Where fish wear pajamas in shades of blue.
Mermaids sip tea with stars on a log,
While sea slugs play poker with a friendly frog.

The crabs hold a pageant, flaunting their claws,
With the starfish cheering, fully in applause.
A wise old turtle shares riddles with flair,
As the waters sparkle, floating in air.

There's a treasure chest bursting with pies,
That jellyfish serve with a twinkling sigh.
The dolphins chat about dreams they had,
In this wacky kingdom, every day's rad!

When the ocean's asleep, the fun stays awake,
With sea cucumbers telling the best jokes to quake.
In this invisible realm, endless smiles bloom,
As laughter pulses, dispelling all gloom.

## Depths of Enchantment

Deep in the blue where the laughter roams,
Merfolk throw parties in their sea foam homes.
A dance-off erupts with the fish and their tails,
While seahorses bop to the beat of the gales.

The shells are storytellers, spinning their yarns,
While clams bake cookies and flounders bake tarts.
Worms ride the currents in waves of delight,
As stingrays zip in a game of kite.

Bubbles are balloons floating high and bright,
As sea stars throw wishes into the night.
The laughter of creatures fills every inch,
In a world where even sea cucumbers clench.

So here in the depths, where enchantment knows,
Mirth paints the sea in colorful prose.
With humor aplenty in this joyous break,
Where the heart of the ocean is wide awake.

## The Language of the Waves

The waves gossip with fish in a whirl,
Telling tales of a mermaid's twirl.
A crab joins in with a clap of claws,
While dolphins giggle at their own flaws.

Octopus ink spills the juiciest news,
A seaweed dancer sways in bright hues.
Jellyfish float with a graceful jab,
Chasing sea turtles, who just want a crab!

Clams chat quietly, knack for a rhyme,
While plankton jiggle through the sands of time.
A whale's good joke echoes far and wide,
As a sea horse winks, oh what a ride!

Bubbles pop like laughter in the blue,
The sea breeze carries humor anew.
With every splash, there's a giggly cheer,
Life under the waves is the best, my dear!

## Underwater Reverberations

Under the waves where the sunbeams dance,
Fish throw a party, if you take the chance.
The sea floor shakes with a playful beat,
As turtles take turns showing off their feet.

A friendly seal tries to balance a ball,
While seahorses giggle, having a ball.
The starfish wave like they're on a stage,
While conch shells gossip, turning the page.

Sardines swirl in a shimmering ball,
Their synchronized moves are a sight to enthrall.
A narwhal fakes hiccups with style and grace,
Causing a fish to roll in place!

With laughter echoing through bubbles so bright,
The ocean sings songs well into the night.
Underwater shenanigans never grow old,
In this fun-filled kingdom where stories unfold!

**Currents of Reflection**

Currents swirl with a joke or two,
As a pufferfish shares his point of view.
The anglerfish flicks his light with flair,
While crabs tell tall tales about the fair!

A deep-sea diver chuckles in surprise,
At the sight of a fish with googly eyes.
Anemones wave as if to say "Boo!"
While jellyfish bob by with a grin or two.

The coral reefs chuckle, a riotous scene,
As clownfish joke like they've trained in a routine.
Every splash pulses with whimsical flair,
In this comedic aquatic affair!

With a wave and a wink, the ocean laughs loud,
In its shimmering depths, fun's always allowed.
So join in the laughter, take a sweet spin,
Where joy flows freely and silliness wins!

## Symphony of the Sea

The sea sings an anthem with bubbles galore,
As dolphins beat drums on the ocean floor.
A sea turtle whistles a melodious tune,
While fishes harmonize under the moon.

A crustacean solo with a pinch and a clap,
Makes the mussels giggle, it's quite the mishap!
Barnacles chime in with a rasp and a cheer,
Creating a symphony for all to hear.

Mackerel swoop in for the grand finale,
With sea urchins dancing in a merry rally.
The ocean's vast stage, where humor's a must,
Crafts a concert of chuckles in shimmer and rust.

As tides rise and fall, let the laughter resound,
In the symphony of life, joy can be found.
So tune in to nature, let senses be free,
For the funny, wild magic of the deep sea!

# Reflections in Aquamarine

In waters bright with silly fish,
A starfish dreams of being swish.
He twirls and spins in bright ballet,
While seahorses cheer him on with sway.

A crab in shades of purple hue,
Wears a hat that's far too blue.
He scuttles sideways, quite the sight,
Flipping past a lamp, oh what a fright!

The jellyfish with tentacles wide,
Took a ride on a grumpy tide.
Bouncing high, he starts to squawk,
Says, "Next time, I'll just take a walk!"

Amidst the laughs of waves that churn,
The clams share tales that twist and turn.
While fish flash smiles, their gills a-whir,
In this silly world, all is a blur.

## The Depths Sing Softly

The octopus plays a ukulele,
Singing tunes that sound quite crazy.
His eight arms strum with such delight,
Even anglerfish can't help but bite!

A whale nearby joins in the fun,
Blowing bubbles, on the run.
With laughter echoing through the blue,
They spread giggles like morning dew.

Hermit crabs dance in tiny shoes,
Swapping shells like fashion news.
They twirl in circles, such a blast,
Who knew shells could be so fast?

As schools of fish parade with style,
Their rainbow colors make us smile.
In this underwater comedy scene,
Every creature joins, small or keen.

## **Cradle of the Sea**

Anemones wave to every passerby,
While a dolphin leaps to touch the sky.
With a splash and a giggle, the sea otters play,
Rolling and tumbling, all through the day.

The bottom dwellers boast their bling,
A disco party is what they bring.
With a clam that raps and a shrimp that sings,
You'd think the ocean has all the things!

A pufferfish puffed up with pride,
Optimistic about his floaty ride.
He met a grouper who tells corny jokes,
Both bursting with laughter, two silly folks.

A parrotfish brightens the scene so vast,
Painting the reef with strokes that last.
In a cradle of giggles, they all convene,
Every finned friend joins this fun routine.

## Hidden Treasures of the Deep

In a kelp forest, a treasure chest hides,
But it's filled with socks, oh what a surprise!
The fish wear them like ponchos in glee,
Fashion-forward under the sea!

A shark with a grin gives a cheeky wink,
While munching on sandwiches (no time to think).
He's convinced that lettuce is quite the steak,
But the ocean's cuisine is a big mistake!

As crabs host a dance with a wiggly worm,
They shimmy and shake with unending charm.
The sea turtle judges with a funky hat,
Says, "You dance like my grandma, imagine that!"

Hidden treasures that bring pure cheer,
In the watery world where laughter steers.
Every fin and shell brings a giggle or two,
In this place where the silly fish flew!

## Marine Serenade

In a realm where fish dance and twirl,
Sardines wear hats and dolphins whirl.
Sea cucumbers gossip, oh what a sight,
Anemones giggle, tickled with light.

Crabs wear sunglasses, sunbathing in style,
Octopuses juggle, it makes them smile.
The seaweed sways in a funky groove,
As clownfish cheer, making moves that soothe.

Starfish play tag on the ocean floor,
While turtles debate the best snacks to score.
A seahorse sings with vocal flair,
While jellyfish spin like they just don't care.

Bubbles float up, like laughter so loud,
Under the waves, a curious crowd.
They share silly secrets, sparkle and gleam,
In this wacky world, where sea creatures dream.

## Echoing Through the Blue

In the depths where the echoes play,
Whales tell jokes in a watery way.
Fishy puns ripple, tickling gills,
As laughter rides on the ocean's frills.

Bubbles burst with a gurgle of cheer,
Crabs crack up with a wave of a claw, dear.
The pufferfish puff and giggle with glee,
As clownfish prank, oh what a spree!

A sea turtle chuckles at a passed-by shell,
Says, 'You look just like me! Isn't that swell?'
Eels slide in with a wiggly dance,
While coral reefs sway, lost in a trance.

Under the shimmer of sun's golden beams,
The sea comes alive with whimsical dreams.
They're a comedy act, all nature's delight,
Echoing giggles resound through the night.

**The Soul of the Sea**

With a tap of a fin and a flip of a tail,
The creatures gather for a laughter-filled tale.
A squid tells stories of adventures so grand,
While shells clink together like a band.

A hermit crab shimmies, showing his shell,
Dancing around like he knows it too well.
Octopus jugglers put on a show,
Throwing clams higher, flawless in a row.

The sea stars twinkle, shining so bright,
As they cheer on the fish in a silly fight.
Tangs twirl and spin, all in good cheer,
"What's the ocean's joke? It's all quite clear!"

Seahorses giggle, keeping it neat,
Swaying with rhythms of a vibrant beat.
In the heart of the blue, where the laughter flows,
The soul of the sea endlessly glows.

## Guardians of the Depths

In the mysteries where the bubbles blurt,
Lobsters hold meetings, wearing theirirt.
They plot funny schemes under shiny waves,
With tales of treasure and silly braves.

Sea otters juggle, like pros on their backs,
While fish in tuxedos dance in flacks.
The seagrass giggles, swaying with mirth,
In the depths of delight, they know their worth.

Jellyfish float by, in their translucent gowns,
Announcing the latest in ocean-bound clowns.
A parade of creatures, all eager to cheer,
At the silliest show each time it draws near.

So here, below where the sun rarely beams,
Guardians of laughter fulfill their own dreams.
With playful abandon, they revel with glee,
In the laughter and joy, forever carefree.

## Depths of Solitude

A clam turned to me with a grin,
Said, "Life's a beach, let the laughter begin!"
The fishes all swam in a comedy show,
While the octopus danced, putting on quite a show.

A jellyfish juggled with quite a flare,
Tangled a seaweed wig in mid-air.
The crabs clapped their claws in delight,
As the sea cucumber took off, quite a sight!

With bubbles and giggles, the tide ebbed away,
Dolphins teased seahorses all through the day.
A whale popped a joke that was so deep,
Even the starfish rolled, trying to keep.

So here in this realm, where the currents play,
Every creature's silly in its own funny way.
Beneath a sea of laughter, oh what a scene,
Even the barnacles dance to the marine!

## Marine Dreams Unraveled

One day a crab donned a party hat,
With a cake made of ocean, imagine that!
He waved to a fish nibbling on a snack,
"Join my bash or you'll miss the fun on this track!"

The oysters played cards, it was quite a sight,
Shells open, they laughed late into the night.
A dolphin, with flair, did a twirl and a spin,
"Who needs a stage when the sea is our den?"

The seahorses polkaed, a wild little dance,
While the sea turtles joined in, given the chance.
A conch blew its horn, very offbeat,
Creating a symphony no one could beat!

So in these waters, with glee all around,
Our dreams swirl like currents, so blissfully bound.
Each ripple a giggle, each wave holds a grin,
In this underwater world, let the laughter begin!

## In the Heart of the Sea

In the heart of the sea, where the laughs bubble up,
A wise old fish sipped from a kelp-filled cup.
He told tales of mermaids with silly pink hair,
That flossed with the waves, oh what a strange pair!

With the shrimp doing limbo under coral beams,
And the plankton twinkling like burst of dreams.
Anemones giggled, shaking their bright heads,
As the pufferfish puffed out in fits of dread!

"Why so serious?" the clownfish declared,
"Embrace this wild rollercoaster, unprepared!"
The sea horse chuckled, said, "Life's quite a jest,
We're just here swimming, so give it your best!"

So down in these depths, with laughter and cheer,
Every creature's a comedian, never a fear.
In the heart of the sea, where we dance and collide,
Every wave's a giggle, like a buoyant tide!

## **Coral Reveries**

Under corals bright, in a carnival twist,
Fish form a conga line, you get the gist!
With a wink and a splash, they shimmy and sway,
In this vibrant parade, they're ready to play.

A pufferfish plumped up and burst out a joke,
"Why did the shark cross the reef? Just to poke!"
The turtles all chuckled, their shells patting sides,
As they floated on currents, embracing the tides.

Clams played charades, in their shelly attire,
Exaggerating moves, it sparked quite the choir.
A dolphin whistled in perfect, sharp tune,
As the eels electric danced 'neath the moon!

So revel, oh fishes, as the sea hums along,
It's a quirky adventure where everyone belongs.
In coral reveries, where silliness reigns,
The laughter goes deep, like the oceanic plains!

# **Currents of Forgotten Dreams**

A crab wearing glasses, quite the sight,
Told me jokes that made the seaweed light.
The fish giggled, shook their fins with glee,
While the octopus danced, a waltz in spree.

Sea turtles played poker, a critical game,
Betting on bubbles, oh what a claim!
A swordfish bluffed, but he wasn't so slick,
Turns out his hand was just a cheap trick.

Anemones whispered secrets in the tide,
As seahorses twirled, full of ocean pride.
But no one believed that there'd be a villain,
Just a lonely puffer, in need of some fillin'.

Jellyfish floated, all sheer and bright,
Playing tag with the rays of light.
With currents that spiraled, and laughter galore,
The treasures of fun were washed ashore.

## Heartbeats of the Blue

A dolphin named Dave, with a laugh so loud,
Told tales of the sea, and drew quite a crowd.
With bubbles for notes, he sang like a star,
"Come join my band, we'll rock from afar!"

A clam joined in, with a shell as a drum,
Tapping out rhythms, making all of us hum.
While fish in tuxedos did a quick jive,
Creating a scene that felt oh so alive.

The seaweed swayed to the beat of the tide,
Whispers of giggles, where joys often hide.
With the sun playing peek-a-boo overhead,
We boogied together, in laughter we fed.

A crab with a hat, looking stately and grand,
Challenged a seahorse to a one-man band.
And in the end, in the bubbles so bright,
We all shared a dance, under the moonlight.

## Depths of Hidden Wonders

In the coral caverns where the sunbeams play,
Lived a starfish who dreamed of Broadway.
With a dazzling smile and a sparkly flair,
He'd sing to the shrimps, put on quite a rare.

A fish in a tutu pranced with delight,
Twirling and whirling, a thrilling sight.
They all took a bow, but oh what a flop,
When an eel made a joke, and they nearly dropped.

Anglerfish stood by, all grumpy and moody,
Telling the others to stop being so goofy.
But a jellyfish tickled his fins with a grin,
And soon all was laughter, even with him in.

The crabs threw confetti from shells all around,
As bubbles of joy in the day were found.
In the depths of the waves, where the laughter swells,
These creatures remind us of magical spells.

## The Language of Waves

Waves whisper jokes as they crash on the shore,
"Why did the dolphin go back for more?"
"Because it saw a fish wearing sneakers!" They said,
And laughter erupted, enough to spread.

The shells held their ears, trying hard not to laugh,
As tide pools spilled secrets in a bubbly half.
"Did you hear about the crab, so very bold?
Tried stealing a shoe, but it wasn't pure gold!"

Octopuses painted great murals on sand,
With colors and swirls that were simply grand.
They'd boast of their talent when asked to compete,
But could never quite sign with those wiggly feet.

Each wave carried stories of revel and cheer,
Echoes of laughter, oh so crystal clear.
In the frothy embrace, where the silly seems grand,
The waves hold a comedy that's utterly planned.

www.ingramcontent.com/pod-product-compliance
Lightning Source LLC
Chambersburg PA
CBHW060143230426
43661CB00003B/546